Online Business

How
To Make Money Online

Learn How to Start An Online Business For FREE:
www.lacobizonlinebusiness.com

© Copyright 2016 by LacoBiz - All rights reserved.

This document is geared towards providing exact and reliable information in regards to the topic and issue covered. The publication is sold with the idea that the publisher is not required to render accounting, officially permitted, or otherwise, qualified services. If advice is necessary, legal or professional, a practiced individual in the profession should be ordered.

- From a Declaration of Principles which was accepted and approved equally by a Committee of the American Bar Association and a Committee of Publishers and Associations.

In no way is it legal to reproduce, duplicate, or transmit any part of this document in either electronic means or in printed format. Recording of this publication is strictly prohibited and any storage of this document is not allowed unless with written permission from the publisher. All rights reserved.

The information provided herein is stated to be truthful and consistent, in that any liability, in terms of inattention or otherwise, by any usage or abuse of any policies, processes, or directions contained within is the solitary and utter responsibility of the recipient reader. Under no circumstances will any legal responsibility or blame be held against the publisher for any reparation, damages, or monetary loss due to the information herein, either directly or indirectly.

Respective authors own all copyrights not held by the publisher.

The information herein is offered for informational purposes solely, and is universal as so. The presentation of the information is without contract or any type of guarantee assurance.

Learn How to Start An Online Business For FREE:
www.lacobizonlinebusiness.com

The trademarks that are used are without any consent, and the publication of the trademark is without permission or backing by the trademark owner. All trademarks and brands within this book are for clarifying purposes only and are the owned by the owners themselves, not affiliated with this document.

Learn How to Start An Online Business For FREE:
www.lacobizonlinebusiness.com

Table of Contents

Chapter 1: Fire Your Boss – Break Free From the 9-5 Grind 6

Chapter 2: Where to Begin? 10

Chapter 3: Affiliate Marketing 23

Chapter 4: Kindle Publishing 34

Chapter 5: Social Media Marketing 40

Learn How to Start An Online Business For FREE:
www.lacobizonlinebusiness.com

WAIT!!! Before you go on and read my book. I would like to thank you for downloading this book. I also want to share with you my own experience and how to start a successful online business from scratch.

Are you tired of not know what to do or where to begin? Please visit my website and I'll share with you everything I know, just follow the link below:

www.lacobizonlinebusiness.com

Chapter 1: Fire Your Boss – Break Free From the 9-5 Grind

Ever imagined how life could be if you made money on your own terms without being a slave of time to boost some company's annual turnover or net profit? Don't you feel sick every Sunday evening when you realize you have to wake up to a job you hate the next morning?

How would you feel if you had greater lifestyle freedom, creativity, higher income and more time with your family? How would you feel if you had the power to choose when to work and when to simply take off for a trek in the mountains? How would you feel if you could actually work anywhere from a cruise to a swanky five star property?

Online businesses give you all of this and more. They rescue you from the 9-5 grind and help you enjoy a life of freedom and fulfillment. Online ventures also allow you to think beyond the "bucket carrying" syndrome to build a pipeline of passive income.

In tradition jobs, your earnings are proportionate to the time you invest in your job. You put in a fixed number of hours, and get paid for those many hours. However, in passive income ventures, you create virtually inexhaustible sources of income and get paid far more than the time and effort put into it. For instance, you research and write an eBook once, and get paid a royalty amount each time someone purchases it. Similarly, you create a valuable blog resource on a specific topic, and keep enjoying advertising or affiliate marketing income on it for years.

Online businesses do not bind your life in time. Sometimes, you have all the money in the world to enjoy the finer things in life, but you are so busy making that money that you lose out on the time to enjoy it. Other times, you have all the time in the world to enjoy the good things in life, but no money for spending in leisurely pursuits. Online businesses can give you true financial freedom, which is having both the time and money to enjoy life.

Online ventures free up your time and give you absolute control of your income and life. Bucket carriers or traditional job holders go to work each day and get buckets of water proportionate to the time spent filling the buckets. Pipeline creators, on the other hand, create pipelines just once and enjoy gushing water into their homes for a lifetime. This is the power of passive income and online ventures. It helps you create wealth streams that operate without having to physically go out there and spend time and effort to make money. It just takes some initial time and effort to build a solid pipeline, whose rewards can be reaped for long.

We pay the price of job security with our financial freedom. In our bid to be "financially secure", we give up our true financial freedom, which is time and money to live life to the fullest. We get trapped in a fear syndrome and keep slogging hard to make money without realizing the long term price we are paying for that so-called security. It has been rightly said that the biggest risk in life is to take no risk.

Can you simply take off for a holiday in a traditional job without squabbling with your boss for leaves? Don't you just want to quit from the painful monotony of the cubicle? Do you really want to be able to work from virtually anywhere in the world and still enjoy a steady stream of income that just keeps growing? Have

Learn How to Start An Online Business For FREE:
www.lacobizonlinebusiness.com

you like millions of others given up your childhood dreams and replaced them with more "realistic" jobs?

The vitality, enthusiasm and passion of our existence is gradually sucked from our souls until our lives are nothing but microwave meals, Netflix binge watching, void dreams and pessimistic Facebook updates about monstrous Monday mornings, non gratifying relationships and uninspiring daily routines. Is this life? Not if you choose to chuck this monotonous and seeming "secure" life.

You realize this is not your complete potential. You are simply settling for something that does not give you deep satisfaction because others are doing it, because you are expected to do it or because you do not think there is any other way. This is nothing but learnt or conditioned helplessness. Know the chained elephant syndrome? Elephants in Africa are tied to a tiny tree with a rather thin rope. The elephant can very easily escape by severing the rope or deracinating the tree. However, it never attempts to break free by doing this.

The elephant's mind has been so conditioned to believe it is not powerful enough to escape that is does not make even the smallest attempt to gain freedom. The powerful, strong and gigantic creature is bound by its own self-limiting beliefs and doubts of its abilities. We are no different from the elephant. We can gain complete financial freedom and create wonders by breaking free from the shackles of the 9-5 grind. Yet, our conditioned thought process and self limiting beliefs prevent us from making an attempt to break free.

Living life on your own terms is the ultimate dream for every individual. The best part is, it is absolutely achievable. Facing your fears and destroying them is the first step towards leading a rewarding life. Rather than indulging in a marathon Netflix watching session, divert your attention elsewhere. Read, learn and create. Identify topics that fire you up. Start building online businesses that become formidable sources of wealth forever. Imagine how wonderful it would be if you did not have to worry about your next paycheck for clearing pending bills or could buy stuff without bothering to look at the price tag.

How can you make a living doing what you absolutely love doing? Where can you start if you want to build an online business? How can you live life on your own terms without being answerable to a boss from hell? How can you build your own money making blogs and websites?

What are some solid online money making ideas? How can you avoid fake online gurus? How to make it big in the competitive world of social media marketing and Kindle publishing? The book lists almost everything a beginner or even experienced marketer needs to know about creating and running successful online business ventures. Start living or die trying – the choice is yours.

Ready to start your own online business? Follow the link below:

www.lacobizonlinebusiness.com

Chapter 2: Where to Begin?

The online world is an inexhaustible money making minefield if you know the right strategies, tools, platforms and resources. The medium can be brilliantly used to target customers from anywhere in the world, while giving you the freedom to operate from any corner of planet earth. The sheer information overload when it comes to setting up an online business can overwhelm and scare the shit out of beginners. How does one select the right niche/topic for a blog? How to put together a comprehensive business plan? How can you monetize your blog or website?

This becomes all the more marked with fake online gurus peddling absolute junk wrapped in shiny paper. They promise you the moon and stars. They position themselves as the ultimate experts with access to some secret Google or Facebook marketing sauce. They are the "marketing authorities" who do nothing but rip you off your hard earned money. These folks are experts yes – experts in emptying bank accounts.

It is easy to spot these pseudos with some practice. Marketing gurus will make you a victim of the shiny object syndrome. They will promise exaggerated and unrealistic results, make tall claims about their income generating system, promise get rich quick results, and teach you to bend the system unethically.

When you sign up for one of the fake marketing guru courses, rather than teaching you the entire money making system, they will teach you a few superficial and on the surface tricks. You are pretty much on your own after they get your money. There's little technical support or idea generation guidance after that.

Do not sign up for anything that promises instant riches. There is nothing like getting rich overnight unless you plan to rob a bank. Solid, dependable and long lasting income streams need effort. Do not let anyone tell you otherwise. Anyone promising to help you make a million dollars in a couple of weeks is obviously a sham. Go for people who set realistic expectations than blatantly exaggerated promises.

Do not opt for any course that teaches you to tweak the system unethically. These gurus encourage you to resort to shortcuts, use unscrupulous means and sometimes even illegal channels to make money online. Is this really how you want to build a fortune? Do you want to give up your 9-5 grind only to land up on the wrong side of the law?

One of the sure shot indicators of a scammy marketing guru is when their website does not list clear contact information. Does it look like it is going to be a challenge to contact them? When they make it tough for you to contact them by not listing basic contact details, it may most likely be a shady venture.

Genuine internet marketers will avoid using a lot of technical and industry jargons to communicate their authority. They do not use hype to impress you and generate a few quick sales. Their testimonials rarely over praise their services to the sky. Fake gurus, on the other hand, have a pool of fake testimonials that sound the same. They rarely mention the credentials or details of people who have written these testimonials for you to verify their authenticity.

Fake gurus can often be spotted by the worthlessness of their information. They make irresistible offers to sell you books or courses that can claim to teach you little known techniques about making money online quickly. You are sold to their promises and buy an eBook about social media or email marketing, only to discover that the information is nothing but generic stuff that is widely available on the internet for free. Getting food out of an alligator's mouth will be easier than trying to apply the "absolutely risk free money back guarantee" for retrieving your funds.

Before purchasing an online training program or business, check its credentials on sites such as WhoIs, Better Business Bureau and Ripoff Report. You can also browse through detailed reviews on various online business blogs and scam alert websites. Always be on guard and avoid falling for the wrong type of online business that will put you off internet ventures forever.

Save time and money. All the research is on this website: www.lacobizonlinebusiness.com

At the onset let's make it clear that though online businesses have a clear edge over traditional jobs when it comes to freedom, flexibility and income creation, it is not a get rich quick overnight scheme. It can be a get rich sure business if you give it the right amount of time, effort and dedication. Online ventures need time and effort but the results can be more than worth it. Imagine setting up a blog by investing time and work initially and then using it as an avenue to make money on autopilot without even looking at it for days together. How will if feel when you come back from a holiday only to find your account pumped up with a few thousand dollars? That feeling!

So now that we know how to spot a scammy turkey from a real business opportunity, how do we go about building an online venture from scratch?

Start here: www.lacobizonlinebusiness.com

The Roadmap to Building Profitable Online Businesses

Create a Business Plan

Every business begins with a solid and comprehensive business plan. Yes, you will obviously be making certain changes later as your enterprise evolves. However, you need a clear objective before starting.

Your business plan should include a clear business or revenue generation model. Are you going to launch an ecommerce venture or will you be starting with a no-frills blog to build a dedicated audience traffic for affiliate marketing or advertising programs such as Adsense? What is your business model? How do you plan to earn revenue through it? If you plan to launch a few affiliate marketing blogs, will you be selling your own information products such as eBooks, email courses and site memberships on it as well?

Do a SWOT analysis of the business. How do you plan to fund your venture? Also, a thorough market analysis is important. Is there a clear demand for your niche? Have you done sufficient keyword research to determine if users are indeed interested in your product/service/ blog topic? Here are some questions that need to be answered in your business plan once you zero down on a topic.

What are the most compelling problems of your customers or target audience? What is your solution for the problem in terms of content or product or service? How are you going to make money solving your audience's problems? What is your target market? Who is your target customer and what is your customer volume? What is the clear competitive advantage you have over similar businesses? Who are your immediate competitors? What are they doing to increase their audience base and buyers? Do you have a ready financial summary? What are your funding sources?

Find a Lucrative Niche

Do you have passion or exceptional expertise in a particular field? It can be anything from child psychology to philately. Can you use your knowledge or passion to target a specific, information or solution hungry market? Niche or topic selection can be the single most important determinant of whether you will create a profitable online business venture or a cold turkey like several others. You need a focused and specific topic to create a revenue generating blog or website.

You may have a passion but may not be sure about how it can be monetized or you may not be able to zero down on a single niche since you consider yourself a jack of all trades. However proficient you are in multiple subjects, focus on a single niche in the initial stages of your online existence. Try to narrow it down as much as possible to dominate the tapered sub-niche. For example, there are tons of luxury travel sites out there, which already have an established customer base and are making tons of money. Now unless you have something really different to offer (which isn't very likely), you are not going to dominate the luxury travel market.

However, there are still plenty of sub niches or sub topics within the broad topic of luxury travel that can be explored. This helps you dominate a single sub niche or laser targeted audience. In the above context, you could come up with sub-niches such as luxury Caribbean honeymoons or luxury pet travel or luxury gay travel. Get the gist? You aim to become the big fish in a small pond rather than a negligibly small fish in the ocean.

Niches are everywhere. Explore your passions, education qualifications, special skills and abilities. Go to Amazon or Clickbank to find the season's hottest niches. Look at the magazines in your local store for inspiration. Google Trends is a great place for grabbing sizzling hot and trending niches. Flippa, a website brokerage site, is another wonderful place for tracking niches that are in demand. Magazine.com and eBay are also worth looking at while brainstorming for a profitable niche.

An expert and little known niche selection tip is to use the power of Google suggest for generating money making niches. For instance, if you want to enter the overcrowded arena of weight loss for women, simply type weight loss for women in Google search. Do not hit enter. Now, check out the suggestions Google comes up with.

It may throw up suggestions such as weight loss for women after pregnancy or weight loss for women after menopause or weight loss pills for women over 30 etc. You will gather some killer sub-niche ideas based on these suggestions. This is the information people are actually looking for.

Google Keyword Planner tool is another niche treasure house. You can enter a broad keyword for it to suggest several other relevant keywords or even utilize it for evaluating other websites to check for keywords that rank well. Another handy niche generation resource is 43Things.com. It lists problems and challenges folks face and things they want to enhance or change in life. When you indentify stuff people want to improve at, you are holding the key to a highly profitable potential market.

Is There An Audience or Competition?

Obviously, even a niche you have remarkable expertise in or are passionate about has to have an audience for you to make money from it. You need data to analyze your audience and future competition. Again, Google is your best friend. Put your existing niche ideas in the Google Keyword Tool to find out if it is a desirable niche. You will gather reference data about the number of searches performed for the keyword each month. Aim for keywords that have global searches between 10,000 to 50,000 a month. So say a keyword such as medieval swords that receives 9,900 searches may be worth exploring.

Domain Name and Hosting

Opt for a brand-able, memorable and unique domain name from a reputed domain registrar such as NameCheap or GoDaddy. Keep it simple and original. Avoid using characters such as dots or dashes in domain names. The extension should preferably be a .com as it is the most widely recognized extension throughout the web world. If not available, you can opt for a .net or .org domain extension.

The actual value is in a .com domain though. You may also want to pick the option of keeping your domain name private, which means your private name, address and contact details will not show up in a public whois.net search. You can include a location or keyword if it is a local business. Keyword dominated domains may not be as effective for optimizing search results but they can make your blog or site more identifiable. You can create a combination of keyword and brandable domain names for best results.

Select a good hosting service based on solid after sales support. Server reliability and uptime score should be one of the most important factors for picking a web host. You need a solid hosting service that operates 24 x 7 on powerful servers and reliable network connections. Your host's uptime score should be above 99.5%. Anything under 99% should be avoided.

Shared hosting can work well for supporting a decently optimized WordPress site with around 30,000 to 40,000 unique monthly visitors. For a beginner, it may be a good idea to start with shared hosting. However, if your website is expected to grow exponentially within the next couple of years, pick up a host that allows you sufficient room for growth.

You should be able to easily upgrade to a dedicated server for faster processing, larger memory, greater disk storage and higher security features. If you are planning to accommodate additional domains, you need more hosting space. Opt for a web hosting service that permits adding several domains.

Another factor to consider is upfront and renewal hosting charges. Some companies offer cheap signup rates only to inflate them during renewal. As a thumb rule, shared hosting should set you back by under $10. However, that budget may have to be notched up a bit if you are looking for additional features. To avoid unpleasant surprises, go through the terms of service and check renewal prices. Go with a service that offers a 30-day money back guarantee so there is zero risk if you are not happy with the service or change your mind.

Does your hosting plan come with superior technical support? What are the different ways through which you can reach them for instant technical support? Keep your eyes open for reviews and feedback. Select hosting firms that offer not just standard customer service but high quality support. Remember – the four key determinants of a hosting service are flexibility, dependability, price and quality.

Learn How to Start An Online Business For FREE:
www.lacobizonlinebusiness.com

Setting Up a WordPress Site

WordPress is one of the most widely used platforms for setting up a blog or website, owing to its flexibility, beauty, customization and tons of features. You do not have to be a web design or programming ninja to create stunning websites with WordPress. It is as simple as selecting the right templates, clicking a few customization options, writing content and publishing it.

It is always good to opt for a self hosted option on Wordpress rather than a free WordPress hosted blog if you planning to make money from it. You will not be able to include banner advertisements or affiliate marketing links on WordPress hosted sites. The URL will be https://weddingfavors.wordpress.com instead of https://www.weddingfavors.com, which takes away from the professionalism of your blog. You can test the waters with a free domain but any serious money making venture will require a self hosted domain.

Pick a Suitable Theme

Standard WordPress themes can work for a basic blog or website. However, you may need a professional looking theme to add more punch to your blog. Premium design themes can be sourced from theme providers such as ThemeForest. Select themes that go best with the overall vibe of your niche or topic. You will also need to add a customized header to make your blog more professional looking, unique and brandable. Add a bright and attention grabbing picture or use a customized background shade.

You can also add a blog avatar by going to the Settings – General option in the WP admin panel. The blog icon will be displayed in the address bar in place of the "W" WordPress icon to help visitors identify your blog.

Widgets

Widgets are add-ons that add more features and functions to your blog. WordPress widgets are nothing but tools or feature blocks that perform a very specific function. They were originally made for adding user friendly and simple design or structure control of the blog theme. Widgets can be easily used with a drag and drop function in the widget area. You can access the entire list of widgets available in the Appearance – Widgets section of the admin dashboard.

Content Is King

Sometimes one has to resort to a cliché because nothing else can better describe it. Content is the king. Do not expect a steady stream of loyal visitors if you fail to impress them with unique, valuable, interesting and resourceful content. Write well-researched and high-quality posts that solve a problem, offer ideas or present a different way to do things.

There cannot be a one size fits all rule when it comes to content creation. It will vary depending on the niche, audience type and your writing style. Your content will obviously not be sorted overnight. Quality content creation is a gradual process where your niche and writing style evolves according to the preferences of your audience. When you measure response and analytics, it will be easier to improve content and give your audience what they want.

Make your blog posts interesting and inspiring. It should create value and be life changing (alright, maybe that's an exaggeration but you get the flow right?). Proofread your posts to ensure they are grammatically correct. Make it easy for people to read your posts by balancing white space with chunks of text. Use tables, bullet points, charts, info-graphics, visuals and videos to make your blog posts spectacular. Blow readers away with the utility you offer. You can do all the marketing in the world and not earn a dime if your content is a turkey.

Optimizing Your Blog Posts

When visitors search for specific information on search engines, search engine spiders crawl the entire World Wide Web to find posts that are most relevant to the keywords entered in the search. Due to the vastness of the web, these spiders do not read each word. Instead, they simply scan millions of pages for particular parts such as the headlines, meta description, subheadings, images and more to check if your page matches the entered search.

Use keywords generously throughout the post. Once you have zeroed down on a few relevant keywords, place them strategically in the headings, subheadings, introductory sentence, ending paragraph, anchor text (hyperlink to other pages on the site), title tags and meta descriptions.

If there are too many competitive keywords in the niche, try using long tail keywords for better targeting. These visitors tend to be more pre qualified and focused. This is the type of laser targeted traffic that converts. For example, instead of "acne remedies" (which is huge), you target "most effective natural remedies for adult acne", you will be dominating a highly focused keyphrase. You can use Wordtracker for gaining access to hundreds of long tail keywords based on a primary keyword or phrase.

Learn How to Start An Online Business For FREE:
www.lacobizonlinebusiness.com

Specific, multiword search phrases are easier to rank for than a general single keyword or a two-word search phrase. Hence, "Caribbean luxury vacations for seniors" is far easier to rank for than simply "vacations for seniors."

Stay miles away from keyword stuffing, which is nothing but filling your post pointlessly with keywords to rank higher. It not just annoys blog followers but can also lead to a ban by Google.

Do not forget to optimize images. Each time you upload an image on the blog, include keywords related to the image in the file name. Also, fill the alternate text option with a short yet keyword optimized description.

Meta descriptions summarize your web page in search results. They give readers an idea of what to expect from the page. Though meta descriptions do not determine your page ranking any more, they are still a crucial factor for ensuring a click-through from among the several pages that are displayed on search engine results. Create a powerful, accurate and interesting description to draw your reader's attention. Include your main keyword in the meta description.

Monetizing Your Blog

Reputed advertising programs like as Google Adsense are still a good way to monetize your blog on autopilot. Once you sign up for an Adsense account and set up the relevant code on the blog/website, it is almost a "make money while you sleep" process. Of course, that is not to say that you will start making money immediately or you do not need to work hard on your content. You need top notch content to attract targeted customers and get them to click on your ad links for earning a tiny commission per click, which can add up considerably if you have impressive traffic figures. Keep posting fresh, new and original content that is of interest to your customers, and they will keep coming back for more.

Banner advertisements are another solid source of income. Once you gain flattering traffic figures, you can sell direct advertising space to businesses looking to target your audience. For instance, if you run a home improvement blog, you may want to negotiate with home improvement chain stores or paint companies or contractors for banner advertisements. The biggest advantage of this monetization method is that there are no middle companies involved and you can set your own rates as long as you have exceptional traffic statistics.

Create and sell your own information products, physical products or services. eBooks are in huge demand due to multiple e-reader applications and devices. If you find a particular sub topic or blog gaining popularity, try and create an eBook for readers who want to know more on the subject. For instance, if you run a relationship blog and find that a particular post your wrote on "save your marriage" garnered a lot of positive response, go ahead and create a full-fledged eBook or information report on "save your marriage" and sell it to your readers.

Learn how to create a free website here:
www.lacobizonlinebusiness.com

Chapter 3: Affiliate Marketing

One of the best and most beginner friendly ways to monetize your blog is affiliate marketing. You do not have to create any products or services for profit making. All you are doing is selling someone else's products or services for a commission.

Affiliate marketing is one of the earliest online marketing forms, where you are simply referring a product or service that you think will be valuable for your blog or website readers. If people buy products based on the links on your blog, you get paid a percentage of commission from each completed sale. The commission can be as low as $1 or as high as $ 10000 based on the products/services that are being promoted.

How does one gain a breakthrough in the competitive world of affiliate marketing? How does one stay afloat with tighter legislations and Google's innumerable updates? How can you stay ahead in the game and create a solid source of passive income in years to come? Read on for all the insider information and techniques on conquering affiliate marketing like a boss.

Stay Focused on a Couple of Products

Do not start marketing a hundred products across multiple niches on your blog. Keep it relevant and clutter free by picking only those products that are high quality and offer tremendous value to your readers.

Try to dominate a single niche or a couple of products. Test them over a longer period of time to see how they fare, rather than changing your products or niches every couple of days. It can be tempting to lose focus when you see multiple products on

Clickbank. However, stay focused on one to two products in the beginning.

Opt For Recurring Affiliate Income

Of course, there is not a one size fits all rule. This will largely depend on your niche and the type of services you are promoting. However, recurring affiliate income is a great way to earn commissions on auto pilot.

There are several affiliate programs that help blogs/websites make money for referring customers as long as these customers stay with the business. It goes without saying; the products/services should be of exceptionally high quality for the customer to stick with it. For instance, the popular email marketing tool Aweber offers a 33 percent lifetime commission, which can be highly lucrative.

Both onetime payouts and recurring payouts have their own advantages and disadvantages.

Research Your Audience

You must know your audience in and out if you want to improve your conversion rates and commissions in affiliate marketing. Pick products that are highly relevant to your audience or solve a clear problem for them.

Know their passion, inspiration, fear, aspiration, problems, lifestyle, interests and more. If your blog is about virtual games, it makes more sense to sell XBOX games rather than books or outdoor sports equipments. You more or less know that your target audience is a bunch of gaming geeks who enjoy hardcore and competitive games. Sell gaming products or gaming strategy eBooks to this hungry audience and watch your profits roll.

Think realistically about what your audience is likely to invest in. If your blog is focused on frugal living or saving money, you are not going to witness much success with luxury items such as branded clothes or cruise vacations. Your products should be in harmony with your audience profile and the general tone/topic of your blog to enjoy more sales.

Reviews for Authenticity

One of the best ways to cut your teeth into the seemingly big bad world of affiliate marketing is by writing killer product reviews. Did you know that 88 percent customers trust online reviews on par with personal recommendations? Writing reviews can help boost your sales up to 18 percent?

There's no harm in writing reviews for products you are promoting as long as you make it clear to your audience that you are promoting the product and receive a share from the sale.

Chances are, your audience is already half way through the buying cycle since they are looking for reviews about the product. They may be ready to buy but just researching around to make a final purchase decision. Unbiased, thorough and comparative reviews can help them do just that. Rather than focusing on writing a great review, concentrate on making it real.

Gain in-depth knowledge about your product, know the clear edge it has over other similar products, highlight the strengths but also include weaknesses, if any. Readers will appreciate your honesty and trust future recommendations even more. Rather than selling products, help your readers buy. Help them find good value for their investment. Guide them in making sensible purchase decisions.

Ensure you include a star rating, the product's standout features, the audience who are likely to benefit most from the product and a clear product image.

Understand Legal Obligations

Ensure you are completely aware of your legal obligations while making money from affiliate marketing. Pay close attention to guidelines and compliance areas while conducting online business, especially affiliate marketing. Steer clear from federal law violations or using unethical means for increasing sales. If you are looking to build a long-term, stable and dependable source of income, beating the system will not help.

You are legally obliged to make a full disclosure of your affiliate relationship with the product. Also, get acquainted with the most updated FTC regulations. Talk to a legal expert if you are not clear about your legal obligations for running a completely compliant affiliate marketing business.

If you are forming a blog publishing entity or planning to publish several affiliate marketing blogs under a single publisher name, you may need to file the relevant documents with the state agency responsible for business filings in the United States of America. There may be a business filing fee involved, which differs from state to state. Once you set up an LLC or corporation, you receive a confirmation certificate that authenticates the existence of your business entity.

Obtain your federal tax ID number from IR website. You can also use your Social Security number if you are running a sole proprietor enterprise or a sole-member LLC. Open a business bank account before starting an online business to process transactions through a website, Paypal or any other payment processor.

This isn't related to affiliate marketing but still worth a mention. If you are selling things on the internet, you may have to pay sales tax on transactions in the state where your business is physically present. Again, this varies from state to state, and it is best to discuss it with your state's tax department or a professional accountant or lawyer to know your legal obligations. You may also have to find out if a business license is required to operate in a particular city, state of country.

Since laws vary drastically from nation to nation, it is best to consult professionals and authorities from your country for complete legal know-how about operating an online business in the region.

Link Cloakers to Your Rescue

Get rid of never-ending and hideous looking affiliate marketing links by using link cloakers. They make the affiliate marketing links appear neater and more professional. Also, make your visuals clickable. Do not make it obvious that you are selling something by using ugly hoplinks. Link cloakers are not just aesthetically appealing but also keep your website professional looking without coming across as a hard-selling platform.

Images can lead interested customers to the offer sales page, which makes the buying process even shorter. Imagine being all excited about checking out a product only to be lead to an unattractive looking picture upload page. Isn't it a sure shot mood killer? Your user experience should be nothing short of spectacular.

Industry Jargons Sorted

CPA is the acronym for Cost Per Action, and includes leads, sales or clicking action or a combination of any of these. CPL is

Cost Per Lead, where the company targets generating leads from customers. For instance, a finance company offering loans may be looking for leads of potential customers who are shopping around for the best loan rates. Use anchor text links to embed your link within a specific phrase. For example, if you are trying to sell an eBook for natural acne remedies, you can simply add the affiliate marketing hoplink within the phrase "natural acne remedies ebook" so the reader is taken to the sales page of the product.

CPC is Cost Per Click or Cost Per Conversion. CPA is nothing but cost for every action performed. For example, a program like Adsense pays the publisher a percentage of the income. It is different from CPA in the sense that in CPC the potential revenue depends on the performed action or on the sales number, and in turn, the commissions generated from these particular sales. While CPC creates income on the basis of click ads, CPA works on an action basis. For instance, whenever a sale is generated.

Searching For The Right Affiliate Program

How do you pick the right affiliate program when there are millions of commission based sales programs on the web? Here are some handy pointers. All programs will have different rules such as margins, payouts and other metrics.

Some products have extremely high commission margins, which means you will have to sell only a few of these to make decent income. Other products may have low margins and require a higher sales volume to make decent commissions. Similarly, some programs require your commissions to reach a minimum level before it can be encashed. Ensure you understand these terms correctly before picking the products you want to sell.

Learn How to Start An Online Business For FREE:
www.lacobizonlinebusiness.com

Select products that you have found to be valuable or useful personally. For instance, if your hosting service is really top class, you can sign up as their affiliate and promote it on your blog for other bloggers looking for a good host. Also, always pick products that have good reviews, ratings and recommendations.

Do not opt for fly by night products with inflated commissions only to lose your audience's trust and credibility. Remember, if you are looking to build a long term and sustainable source of income, choose your products carefully. Your readers trust you. They buy based on your recommendations and probably not because of the company. Do not shake your priceless reputation for a few pennies.

On Clickbank, you can select metrics such as "Gravity or "Network Earnings" to know which products are performing really well.

One of the best product selection tips is to buy the product you are recommending to your readers. How will you be in a position to give an honest and unbiased review if you haven't even seen or used the product/service? Lack of details may kill your reviews when people are looking for specifics to make purchase decisions. Readers love minute details, a comprehensive list of features and comparative analysis of products in tabular format.

Sharing your own experience with the product makes the pitch more personal and informed. If there is an eBook that helped you boost your blog earnings, share how it did that. You can create a graph to show the before and after results of reading the book. Readers enjoy reading personal experiences and insights over plain research.

Present information in a manner that helps readers scan for key points and important features quickly to make their decision. Though reviews should be detailed, they should also have tables, charts, key points, summary etc. to help highlight the important points. Avoid giving broad or generic information about the product that can be found everywhere else. The objective is to give your customer everything he needs to make the decision and buy immediately, without wandering anywhere else.

You will learn to identify your winning stallions with trial and error. Find out which products bring you maximum income and chuck out the others. Focus all your efforts on boosting the sales of the winning goods even more by creating more effective and conversion compatible links.

Create Valuable Content

Shift from pay per click marketing strategies and focus on creating high quality content for a laser targeted audience. Deliver content that offers value consistently to readers. Well researched, interesting and information loaded content keeps your visitors hooked. Find topics that are relevant, problem solving and engaging for your readers. Affiliate marketing has evolved from click through sales to building a relationship with your audience by gaining their trust and loyalty.

You should be able to establish a level of comfort, authority and credibility with your audience, before getting them to buy from you. Impress your audience with real and non-fluffy value before they are comfortable for taking action on affiliate links on your blog.

Give your visitors information that equips them with actionable takeaways for making informed buying decisions. Become a valuable resource, a virtual friend they can return to whenever they need guidance about a product or service. This really makes all the difference between people struggling to make affiliate sales and those rolling in millions of dollars worth of affiliate commissions.

Include Personal Bonuses

To make the buying proposition even more lucrative for the buyer, throw in your own bonus in the form of a free course or eBook. The most important thing is to ensure that the product you are offering as a bonus for buying from you is complimentary or related to what the reader is purchasing.

For instance, if your reader is buying a course on "copywriting for blogs", you can throw in a handy blog creation checklist or blog design eBook to help them create more professional looking and sticky blogs. Go through the affiliate program's policies to ensure they allow bonuses for affiliate sales.

It Takes Time To Make Money

Do not give up if you do not make money immediately. You won't have a million visitors wanting to buy from your affiliate link immediately. You have to market your blog well, engage your audience, generate traffic and build trust. These steps can be time consuming and require consistent efforts. It is certainly not an overnight process.

There are many affiliate marketers who make five and six figure incomes from their blogs, and none of them started making money overnight. They focused on creating content and building brands over simply enticing customers to click on worthless links. You will start seeing results gradually as you speed up your efforts.

Avoid Promoting Different Products from the Same Category

Lucrative as it may sound, avoid promoting more than a couple of products from the same category. It makes your stand look more believable. For example, if you keep recommending weight loss pill X for a few days, followed by weight loss pill Y and Z in the next few days, you are confusing your audience. You may have told them why X is the best or why they should buy X, only to end up selling Y and Z later.

The higher the number of products you promote from a single category, the more challenging it is for your audience to make a clear decision. If you consistently promote a single or a couple of products, the readers will come to the conclusion that there might be really something exceptional about the particular product for you to keep at it for so long. This wins their trust in favor of the product you are promoting. On the other hand, they are less likely to take fluctuating product promotions seriously.

Use the Resources Section Resourcefully

Use your resources or tools page ingeniously to promote related products or services. This is not a much used option, though it can be brilliant if you know how to take advantage. This not just helps you promote your products effectively, but is also valuable for readers who are looking for additional resources. They may also come across products they were not originally looking for yet are happy to discover. It is a win-win for everyone involved.

Think Out of the Box

Think out of the box if your niche is too saturated in the online space. Exploit different channels with an existing audience base. For example, if you have a blog related to real estate investment, you can tie up with real estate agents in different cities and work out a pay per lead arrangement with them. You can earn a neat commission each time a visitor looking to invest in a property enters their details. You can create attractive lead based ads, such as "get the best real estate deals in your city" or "check out the best real estate investment options in your city."

If you own a Caribbean travel site, you can tie up with local holiday rental or beach villa rental services. Each time your readers or audience signs up for information on vacationing in the Caribbean or renting a villa there, you can get paid a commission per lead by the rental company. This is a great way to think out of the box and make money from local businesses. The businesses get multiple leads, you earn good commission and customers get what they are looking for.

The skills that you need to succeed is on this website: www.lacobizonlinebusiness.com

Chapter 4: Kindle Publishing

People have taken to eBooks incredibly well, due to its practicality, functionality and flexibility. Publishing on Kindle is one of the best ways to rake in passive income in the online world today. You get access to a worldwide audience base on a reputed platform like Amazon.

People can access your books from just about anywhere on their hand held devices. Plus, the costs of putting together an Ebook is comparatively lesser than other starter ventures, depending on the scale on which you plan to operate. If you have a specific passion or expertise that others might be interested in or are willing to deeply research a problem for which people are constantly looking for solutions, creating eBooks can be a highly lucrative proposition.

Choosing between KDP Select and Kindle Direct Publishing

The first step is to decide whether you want to publish your book on Kindle Select or Kindle Direct Publishing. While publishing on Kindle Select can offer you several additional features and benefits, it also demands exclusivity. If you opt to sell your eBook with Kindle Select, you cannot publish it on another platform.

Both KDP select and Kindle Direct Publishing offer authors a 70 percent royalty for books priced from $2.99 to $9.99. All KPD Select titles can be downloaded from the Kindle Owner's Lending Library. This entitles you to receive a portion of the total monthly earnings on KOLL, which may not be huge but still decent enough if your book witnesses multiple downloads.

Learn How to Start An Online Business For FREE: www.lacobizonlinebusiness.com

Beginners may do well to focus their efforts on a single platform than publishing all over the place. It can help you measure audience response and results more effectively than selling on multiple platforms simultaneously. From this perspective, KDP Select may be a good option for Kindle publishing newbies. However, at the end of the day, you have to decide which channel you want to select based on individual goals, your eBook topic and online business objectives.

Write Your Book

Te first step for writing your book is to create a rough skeleton, which you can later add flesh and bones to. Research topical forums, blogs and social media pages to know the exact concerns or passions of your target audience. Try and structure your table of contents around the most pressing concerns or hot topics.

In the first draft, all you need to do is vomit everything on a blank page. Not the most pleasant way to describe this but you get the flow, right? Just write anything that comes to mind without filtering it. You can create a table of contents and include a brief note/summary of key points to be included in each chapter. Put down all ideas, stories, analogies and ideas you can think of. The objective is to begin and not to make it flawless.

The review draft is where you go about fleshing out the table of contents. You spend time developing what you wish to write and how it should be written. Enlist the help of a few people for feedback and analysis. They may give you constructive feedback from a reader's perspective about what works and what doesn't.

The final draft is your editorial draft, where you hire the services of a professional editor or enlist the help of a linguistically savvy

Learn How to Start An Online Business For FREE:
www.lacobizonlinebusiness.com

friend. They will check the finished product not just for grammar, but also style elements, structure and readability flow.

Design a Stunning Cover

Create a visually stunning, attention grabbing and relevant eBook cover to floor your audience. In a pool of hundreds of titles on similar topics, your cover will help the book stand out. A professional, interesting and resourceful cover inspires readers to find out more about the book. It piques their curiosity and boosts the visual appeal of your product.

Packaging is as important as substance. You may have created the most well-researched and comprehensive book, but if you can't convince your customers to buy the book by packaging it attractively, your efforts are futile. Also, your eBook cover is the sole element to be displayed to readers under the "Customers Who Bought This Item Also Bought" section.

Outsource the creation of your eBook to a professional and experienced graphic designer if you are not proficient in using an image software. Use high resolution 1553 px x 2500px visuals. Keep your colors bright, fonts bold and pictures clear to make a lasting impression on readers.

Publish your eBook

How can you publish a book on Amazon to actually make it accessible to millions of readers? This is the part that scares most folks. However, it isn't as intimidating as it appears. All it takes are a few steps. Here is everything you want to know about publishing your book on Kindle.

1. Sign in with your Amazon account on kdp.amazon.com. Enter your tax details for earning royalties.

2. Click Bookshelf followed by "Add new Title"

3. Fill out all the details about your book including title, a short description and relevant keywords. Incorporate words and phrases that people are most likely to use while searching for your book.

4. Upload your Ebook cover file in JPEG format.

5. Upload your actual book file. Make sure to test view the book on Amazon's online viewer to ensure it looks nice and professional, because this is exactly how it will appear to your readers

6. Next, select "Save and Continue", followed by "Worldwide Rights" on the publishing rights and price page.

7. Choose the 70% royalty price option if you plan to price your books between $2.99 to 9.99. Unless, you have a compelling reason to do so, prices should be kept within this range for maximizing your royalties. Click Save and Publish once you are done selecting your options.

8. Amazon will send you a conformation mail within 24-48 hours (generally happens quicker than that) when the book is ready to go live.

Promoting Your Book

You are all set to shout out loud and tell the planet about your creation. However, you need a few endorsements before you go ahead and do that. Reviews are crucial because they are social validations that lend some legitimacy to your work, especially for new authors.

To bag some starter positive reviews, send a few complimentary copies of your books to family and friends, and ask them to leave detailed reviews in return. StoryCartel.com is a good place for eBook authors to get unbiased, ethical and free reviews. Request your readers to leave genuine reviews. It doesn't have to be all 5-star rated or superficial flattery. An honest critique of your work can lend it a more credible and authoritative touch.

Keep in mind that reviews can be added only a few days prior to book's publishing date on Kindle. Hence, publish your eBook a couple of days before you actually inform everyone about it. This helps you garner early reviews, which boost the product for new readers. After its official release, readers can be directed to the product page where they can check out some glowing reviews before making a purchasing decision.

Also, ensure that you share your book with influencers from your field for their unbiased reviews and recommendations. Influencers are people who wield tremendous power over people's buying decisions due to their large following on social media or blogs and industry expertise. Unbiased and genuine reviews from these influencers can help you bag plenty of early buyers.

Make the proposition of buying your book irresistible by throwing in a time sensitive incentive for early buyers. For instance, Andy Traub made more than $20,000 in 3 months with a single eBook by including an audiobook, a comprehensive 30-day email course and membership to a busy online community with the eBook. Make it an offer people cannot refuse.

Promote your book on the social media by creating a buzz with contests, giveaways and interesting updates that inspire readers to give your book a glance. Social signals or social proof is an important factor for improving your book's organic search engine ranking. Amazon has its own algorithm when it comes to promoting your book in the recommended books section to its audience.

You have to self-promote and hit a specific upfront sales mark for Amazon to pitch in. Also, your books earn an impressively high rank if they are purchased by several buyers at once. The flattering rank can in turn help you sell more books based on the fact that it has been bought by several people.

Get Feedback

What is the general feel about the book among your target audience? Are there any constructive suggestions which can be kept in mind for future titles? What are the things that have appealed to readers who have given your book a four or five star rating?

Why are people enjoying or disliking the book? This isn't for vain flattery but to measure your results, keep track of your performance and incorporate the necessary changes in subsequent books. If you are publishing on multiple platforms, assess how your results on Amazon compare with other platforms.

Here is a comparison between two most reliable and best Kindle Publishing Business program:
www.lacobizonlinebusiness.com/Comparison

Chapter 5: Social Media Marketing

Simply creating products/services/content and offering it to your audience is passé. The real deal today is to leverage the power of social media marketing for engaging your audience, establishing strong connections and building brand credibility/authority.

Social media marketing dramatically decreases your marketing budget by targeting a huge base of focused followers in one go. It boosts your search engine placement ranking with social signals. The more people like, share, retweet and comment on your posts, the higher your social endorsement and brand credibility raises in the eyes of Google.

Social media has revolutionized the way online businesses are conducted by making it more personal, real time and focused. You can laser target social media users based on their interests and preferences, while boosting overall customer experience. You can build authority by creating power-packed content for a hungry audience. What's more? You can have lots of fun while doing so. Here are some of the most solid social media marketing tips to give your online business a clear edge.

Build Communities with Actionable Hashtags

Hashtags go beyond helping users find relevant content based on a topic. Use them for building and creating loyal communities around things people are passionate about. For example, if your blog/website is related to travel, instead of simply creating a #beautifulafrica or #vacationsafrica hashtag for tracking all photographs of Greece, build more meaningful hashtags like #volunteertravelafrica, where users can share their experience or tips on volunteering in Africa and build a strong community feel.

People need to feel a sense of belongingness or part of a community. This fosters greater loyalty and engagement, which in turn gradually converts them into buyers and brand evangelists.

Hashtags can also be used for contests and humor. You can ask your audience on Twitter, Instagram and Facebook to share a picture of themselves enjoying your product or service with the hashtag, and sharing it with their followers to be eligible for the contest. Your hashtag gains more prominence, and quickly goes viral even if a few hundred people share it.

Keep hashtags snappy, memorable and unique. It should be spell easy and catchy. Use the right emotions to evoke the interest of your target audience.

Use Content Management Tools

This is especially useful if you are dabbling in multiple social media platforms. It can be challenging to keep track of your posting schedule, editorial calendar and other content management tasks. Use a program like Hootsuite or Buffer for scheduling your social media posts in a planned and organized manner.

Create an editorial calendar for the week or month, and upload content on the appropriate platform. Save time during the week by scheduling your posts for a couple of hours on weekends.

Post consistently by creating a fixed schedule. You can't post multiple times on a single day and not post at all for the next couple of days. There has to be a pre determined and consistent pattern to your posts. For instance, Facebook and Twitter are really fast and may need more than a single post a day, while Instagram and Snapchat can do with one post a day. Determine the number of posts to be updated on each platform and stick to it.

Focus on Becoming a Resource

Social media is not about hard-selling or aggressively promoting products. Use its power to become the ultimate resource on your topic/niche. It is much easier to sell to an audience who trust you because of the crazy high value you have offered them in terms of content and resources. Do not start selling right away without building connections and engaging your audience.

Write and share posts about things that concern your audience the most. Curate content from other helpful resources for folks who do not have the time to look at multiple pages. Ask readers to private message their questions to you, which you can put on your public page for other readers to answer. Create fun games and contests. Use evocative images with an incomplete tagline for your audience to complete. For instance, there's never a wrong time for --------. People love social media brands that engage them rather than just sell to them.

Make Your Visuals Count

A picture indeed speaks more than a thousand words. Social media is a highly visual medium that thrives of stunning and attention grabbing images. Use eye catching, relevant and high resolution images to complement your posts.

If you are not using your own images, ensure you are legally permitted to use an image. Picking images randomly from Google's image search can get you in legal trouble for copyright violations. Understand the usage rights of every image before including it in your post. Flickr, Pixabay and Wiki Commons can be good places to start if you are looking for free images, though it is recommended that you use your own pictures. Read the rights of each image on these sites before using it.

Another expert tip is to make your images clickable. People love to click on images they enjoy seeing. This can be used to build excitement and lead them to your blog or website to gather more information about your products or services.

Post at the Right Time

If you want a huge audience to be exposed to your updates, post at a time when audience presence is optimal on the platform. For instance, the best time to post on Facebook is from 12:00 p.m. to 1:00 p.m. on weekends, 3:00 p.m. on Wednesdays and 1:00 p.m. to 4:00 p.m. on Thursdays and Fridays.

Early mornings when people are commuting to work and late evenings are also a good time for catching your target audience online. The optimal time for a Twitter post on weekdays is from 12:00 -3:00 p.m. and 5:00 p.m. Pinterest has more female users who are mostly active in the evenings from 8:00-11:00, especially Saturdays. Instagram witnesses a strong audience presence from Monday to Thursday all the time except 3:00-4:00 p.m.

The best time to post on LinkedIn is from 5:00 – 6:00 pm midweek. Another good time to post on it is from 10:00 to 11:00 a.m. on Tuesdays and Wednesdays. On Thursdays it is 7:30 – 8:30 a.m.

It is also a good idea to repeat important posts a couple of times. Some people may have missed it the first time around due to time differences or other factors. Posting it again may expose it to a larger audience, including new followers.

Build Relationships with Other Bloggers to Cross Promote

Engage with people, pages or accounts that belong to your industry to forge greater connections for cross promotion. Leave behind insightful, well researched and thought-provoking comments on similar pages. Share valuable blog posts created by industry authorities in your domain. Respond intelligently and factually to queries put up by readers on other pages.

One solid tip that few experts share with newcomers is to create expert round-ups. For instance, if you are dealing with a post pregnancy and baby care blog, you contact as many experts in early child care and post natal care to feature in your round-up. Each of them can share their best child care or post pregnancy tip on these round ups. This not just helps you create a valuable resource for your readers, but you will also be assured a huge audience. Each of the experts will share the round up with their followers since everyone likes to be tagged as an expert or authority in their domain. So say, "infant nutrition expert round-up- 20 industry experts share their best infant nutrition tips" can work brilliantly for increasing your following.

You can also tag similar pages on your updates. This not just gives exposure to the other pages among your followers, but also helps your posts show up on their pages to pique the interests of their audience. Win-win? You bet.

Another super tip that has become very effective post the reply button option on Facebook is to rope in influencers or industry experts for a question and answer session with your audience. Readers can post meaningful questions, which can be answered by these experts to create an engaging and interactive knowledge resource.

Share Behind the Scenes Stories

Social media is all about adding a human element to your brand. It is about winning your audience by forging personal connections, building relationships and humanizing your brand. What better way to do this than share behind the scenes stories of your blog/brand/organization?

Use platforms such as Instragram, Twitter and Facebook to post images about your journey as a blogger or company. It can be about office celebrations or a lunch out with the team or an outing with a social media follower – just about anything that brings to the fore people behind the scenes to make the process more personal and less promotional.

Your brand recognition, likeability and desirability will climb up several notches to encourage people to buy from you. Humanizing your brand instills a sense of belongingness in your customers. They feel a part of your brand. This reinforces brand loyalty and brings more business your way. Focus as much on engaging existing customers as you do on gaining new followers.

One of the biggest mistakes newbie social media marketers make is concentrating only on gaining a larger following and more likes. Engaging and retaining existing followers is as important as gaining new ones. Social signals are based on your page activity and hence engagement and interactivity are crucial from the organic search perspective.

Activate Similar Page Suggestions

This is a lesser known Facebook marketing tip that few marketers will ever tell you about. If you want to gain lots of free likes, simply enable your "similar page suggestions" option from your page's settings tab. Facebook starts recommending your page to users who like a competitor's page.

Also to boost visibility, go to the "menu" option, and Select "All of Your Friends" instead of "Friends and Pages You Interact with Most." This exposes your posts to all your friends or pages rather than a select group of pages or individuals you frequently interact with.

Leverage the Power of Videos

In the attention deficit internet world, people love to consume quick and interesting videos that are easy to absorb over elaborate text pieces. Use this powerful visual medium to create snappy, attention grabbing and useful videos, and upload them on Facebook, Instagram, YouTube and Twitter.

It can be anything from how to do something quickly to video testimonials of customers/readers who are pleased with your product/service to introducing your employees. Keep the videos natural, fun and personal. Useful, funny and strong emotion evoking content is shared more frequently by social media users.

Offer them solid value so they look forward to subscribing to your channel or sharing your video with their followers. People love to share useful stuff that makes them come across as well-informed, intelligent and smart within their social circle. It is gaining a sort of social currency or endorsement for their awesomeness. Give your followers content that makes them come across as smart among their social circle when they share it. For instance, if you run a cooking blog or business, a video on "how to make a microwave cake in less than 10 minutes" or "5 ideas for quick one pot meals" can trigger your audience's interests.

Check Out Trending Topics

How do you know what topics are massively trending in your niche so you can create similar content around it? Go to Buzzsumo and check out the top shared content pieces on any topic. Once you get to know the type of posts/topics that are performing really well on a particular platform, slay it by creating similar content and add your own unique twist to it. Make it even better than the post that tops the tending chart.

For instance, if you run a business or blog related to baby and infant care, and you note that the most extensively shared posts are ones about making your own baby food for babies who have just started eating solids, create a killer blog about homemade baby food for infants. Research deeply. Add a few recipes of your own. Tweak existing recipes. Also, now since you know baby food and nutrition is a topic that is of interest to plenty of people, start thinking of content ideas along the line. So say, baby food reviews, nutritional requirement for infants, how to get your baby to enjoy what they eat, inculcating food discipline and other similar topics. You may even plan an entire blog around the topic. This way you take existing popular topics and give them a nice twist to garner loads of likes and social shares.

Look for different content angles if you want to create a distinct identify for your online business. Do not do the hackneyed top 10 lists for the hundredth time. People love originality, novelty and freshness of perspective. If best beach resorts in xyz has been done to death, try to explore best dog friendly beach resorts in xyz or best toddler friendly beach resorts in xyz. Try to

Learn How to Start An Online Business For FREE:
www.lacobizonlinebusiness.com

keep your post more narrowed down and relevant for your target audience rather than making general lists.

Place Social Share Buttons Prominently on Your Blog

If you want your audience to perform a certain action, make it easy for them to do it. Place social buttons conspicuously on your blog or website to increase your following and shares. Use both – "like" buttons (for sharing content) and page plugins (to boost likes and following).

Place the buttons next to your blog post or just under it so people who have enjoyed reading it know what to do next if they want to share the piece. You can also cross promote your social media pages. For instance, your Facebook page can be promoted on your LinkedIn or Twitter profile. People follow you on various networks and become even more exposed to your messages each day.

Create Groups Rather than Business Pages

Create Facebook groups rather than simply creating business or website pages. This way you build a more dedicated community as a prelude to your business. They are also brilliant channels for organic exposure and credibility building. Group members receive a notification each time posts get uploaded. Keep discussions relevant to your industry or blog. Tag active members in a post to engage them in a conversation.

Post news and updates related to your industry. Trigger conversations and discussions that will be helpful for your target audience. For example, if you have a blog related to pet travel, create a group for traveloholics who love vacationing with their pets.

Encourage them to ask questions and position yourself or your employees as the experts who answer these queries. Once group members understand the usefulness of your answers, they will be more likely to click on your profile or business page. This gives your blog or business page more exposure.

Keep Tweets Really Short

One expert tip if you want more retweets is to keep your tweets really short. There is already a stringent character limitation on the platform (140 characters). However, tweets around 110 characters enjoy 17% more engagement. This happens because leaving a few characters in your Tweet makes it easier for people to retweet with their own comment. Ideally, keep your tweets between 75-110 characters.

If all the characters are exhausted, people have to do some editing before retweeting it, which makes it a more time consuming and tiresome process. In general, people will do less of what needs additional effort, and will instead opt for convenient quick fixes.

Create a Distinct Brand Personality

Whether you are on Instagram or Twitter or Pinterest, you need to have a clear and distinct brand persona that strikes a chord with your customers. Business social media accounts are dramatically different from personal accounts. On our personal accounts, we share things randomly without following a specific tone or pattern.

However, brands or businesses possess a consistent, distinct and clear identity that reflects in each post. Do you position yourself as a humorous and fun brand or are you going to adopt a more pensive and somber tone? What is your primary brand personality? Do your posts echo the overall tone or persona of your brand?

Create advice giving content, personal narratives, motivational or inspirational memes, problem solving strategies, personal reflections and much more with the help of powerful images on Instagram. Write insightful, valuable and actionable blogs on Facebook. Focus on building brands than blatantly selling to your audience. Your followers will come to associate your brand with certain values, which in turn will motivate them to buy stuff.

One of the best and easiest ways to know what works and what doesn't is to simply go on a competitor's page and check out what they are doing for their brand building. You can simply mirror their strategies and win over your audience.

Start your online business here:
www.lacobizonlinebusiness.com

Conclusion

Thank you for downloading this book.

I hope the book was able to help you understand the value of working on your own terms and the actual steps required to achieve financial freedom with an online business.

The book is filled with lots of little known strategies, expert tips and actionable points to help you dominate the world of online business and marketing with confidence.

The next step is to simply take action. Do not be bogged down by the analysis paralysis syndrome by reading and analyzing everything, but failing to act on it. An online business is certainly not a get rich quick scheme. However, it is a get rich sure business model if you work hard, are consistent in your efforts and patient with the results.

Lastly, if you enjoyed the book, please take time to share your views by posting a review. I'd be highly appreciated!

Here's to your rewarding, profitable and financially free future.

Don't forget to visit the website:
www.lacobizonlinebusiness.com

www.ingramcontent.com/pod-product-compliance
Lightning Source LLC
Chambersburg PA
CBHW061226180526
45170CB00003B/1182